YOU ARE HELPFUL

WRITTEN BY TODD SNOW
ILLUSTRATED BY MELODEE STRONG

Maren Green Publishing, Inc.
Oak Park Heights, Minnesota

FOR CARMEN'S MOM,
BECAUSE YOU ARE.
-T.S.

TO JEREMY AND HEATHER,
FOR ALL THE TIMES YOU HELPED ME OUT.
THANKS! MELODEE

Ages 4 and up

 Maren Green Publishing, Inc.

5525 Memorial Avenue North, Suite 6

Oak Park Heights, MN 55082

Toll-free 800-287-1512

Text copyright © 2008 Todd Snow
Illustrations copyright © 2008 Melodee Strong

Library of Congress Cataloging-in-Publication Data is available.

Edited by Pamela Espeland
Text set in Garamond Pro and Wonderlism
Illustrations created using acrylic on wood
First Edition November 2008
10 9 8 7 6 5 4 3 2 1
Manufactured in China

ISBN 978-1-934277-23-2 (pbk.)

www.marengreen.com

YOU ARE HELPFUL
IN MANY WAYS.

YOU ARE HELPFUL WHEN YOU GET DRESSED BY YOURSELF.

YOU ARE HELPFUL

wHEN YOu PuT
YOUR TOYS awaY.

YOU ARE HELPFUL WHEN YOU HOLD HANDS.

YOU ARE HELPFUL WHEN YOU DO CHORES

AT HOME.

YOU ARE HELPFUL

WHEN YOU WAIT YOUR TURN.

YOU ARE HELPFUL WHEN
YOU SIT STILL

AND OPEN WIDE.

YOU ARE HELPFUL WHEN
YOU PUT TRASH

IN THE RIGHT PLACE.

PLASTIC

ALUMINUM

TRA

YOU ARE HELPFUL
WHEN YOU LISTEN

AND FOLLOW INSTRUCTIONS.

AND YOU DO.

Also available from Maren Green Publishing

ISBN 978-1-934277-19-5

You Are Brave *By Todd Snow, illustrated by Melodee Strong.* What does it mean to be brave? For children, it can mean meeting new people, trying new foods, and letting friends play with their toys. Each child is brave in his or her own ways. Written in simple words, vividly illustrated with realistic scenes that relate to children's everyday lives, *You Are Brave* lets young children know that bravery is about many things: feelings, actions, and being open to new experiences. *Paperback, full color, 8" x 8", 24 pages. Ages 4 & up.* MG119 **$8.99**
Also available in board book format: Full color, 6" x 6", 24 pages, Ages Baby—Preschool. (ISBN 978-1-934277-08-9) MG110 **$6.99**

You Are Friendly *By Todd Snow, illustrated by Melodee Strong.* Children want to make friends and be friendly. This warm, affirming book helps them build important social skills. Sharing, saying "please" and "thank you," inviting others to join in and play, treating people and animals kindly, and offering to help are all ways to win friends. Written in simple words, vividly illustrated with realistic scenes that relate to children's everyday lives, *You Are Friendly* guides children to create healthy, positive relationships with others. *Paperback, full color, 8" x 8", 24 pages. Ages 4 & up.* MG120 **$8.99**
Also available in board book format: Full color, 6" x 6", 24 pages, Ages Baby—Preschool. (ISBN 978-1-934277-09-6) MG109 **$6.99**

ISBN 978-1-934277-18-8

ISBN 978-1-934277-22-5

You Are Healthy *By Todd Snow, illustrated by Melodee Strong.* Experts have identified key behaviors important to children's health. These include active play, eating right, washing hands, drinking water, getting enough sleep, and spending time with loved ones. This warm, inviting book introduces young children to things they can do to stay healthy and happy. Written in simple words, vividly illustrated with realistic scenes that relate to children's everyday lives, *You Are Healthy* is an ideal introduction to a lifetime of good health. *Paperback, full color, 8" x 8", 24 pages. Ages 4 & up.* MG117 **$8.99**

www.marengreen.com
5525 Memorial Avenue North, Suite 6 • Oak Park Heights, MN 55082
phone 800-287-1512 • 651-439-4500 • fax 651-439-4532 • email orders@marengreen.com